Settling for Beauty

Settling for Beauty

Poems by ~~J.D. Smith~~

J.D. Smith

Cherry Grove Collections

Judy,

Thank you very, very much for your interest and support!

I hope these poems provide some small amount of pleasure.

John

15 October 2005

Published by Cherry Grove Collections
P.O. Box 541106
Cincinnati, OH 45254-1106

Typeset in Garamond by WordTech Communications LLC, Cincinnati, OH

ISBN: 1933456051
LCCN: 2005931941

Poetry Editor: Kevin Walzer
Business Editor: Lori Jareo

Visit us on the web at www.cherry-grove.com

Acknowledgments

Acknowledgment is gratefully made to the following publications in which some of this collection's poems, at times in somewhat different form, appeared: *After Hours*, *Architrave*, *Arkansas Review*, *Barkeater*, *Big Muddy*, *Buffalo Bones*, *Burning Word*, *Concrete Wolf*, *Eleventh Muse*, *Erete's Bloom*, *eye-rhyme*, *Into the Teeth of the Wind*, *Lilliput Review*, *The Lucid Stone*, *Lyric Poetry Review*, *Mediphors*, *Minimus*, *New Delta Review*, *Out of Line*, *Paper Street Press*, *The Pedestal Magazine*, *Potomac Review*, *South Ash Press*, *Stray Dog*, *Texas Poetry Calendar 2003*, *Texas Review*, *Wavelength*, and *WordWrights*.

For friends who have encouraged and waited

Contents

1.

Ars Amoris

Even if you feel prepared to love,
it may be best
to start with something
smaller than humanity
or a lover.
A stone the size of your fist will suffice.
It can be held in one hand,
but not hidden.
Its weight will change your stride.
It can be thrown
no more than a few steps away,
to be found in deep grass
by stubbing your toe.

The stone you choose
should not be porous to persuasion.
It must not glisten with crystal,
glower with obvious ore.
Its stone skin must reflect no light.
Its center—more of the same,
fern-fossil, or agate—
can be revealed only through a fall
from a great height,
or a great hammer's landing,
but to dash this stone
would turn it into another thing,
or things—a hapless plurality,
of gravel, then sand.
To ensconce this stone
in wall or fence, however solidly,
would turn it into a part, a mere means.
But this stone, you decide,
is an end in itself,
its own monument,

marking no mile
and no trail.

You bring the stone inside from the seasons
of prying ice and fevered dew.
To lose a chip is unthinkable.
A scratch is to be mourned.
There is no word from the stone
regarding your devotions,
which means there is work to do:
a place must be cleared on a deep mantle,
a spot in the center of the bed.
When this is done, the stone
will keep its own counsel,
as it has from the start.

Such constancy is a reproach.
How often have you thought
of bus fare, packing a lunch,
of so many things that are not the stone?
You redouble your attentions,
use up your sick days,
then your vacation,
take days off with no excuse
and risk being fired,
in sacrifice to the object
of your love,
with evenings and weekends
to give praise, to hold,
hours of candlelight and roses.
Many pass, and still
the stone is unmoved.
It seems to grow distant.

Watching for its slightest variation,
a return to some orbit of grace
that must have prevailed before,
melts the soul's remaining fat

and leaves you feeding on a single thought
that gives its name
as *to give, to please.*
Then the thought begins to waste,
unfed by fact.
What's left is another thought:
this stone, shaped for someone else's hand,

must be set out for that hand to find.
Laying the stone in a place
of both sun and shade,
you press a thumbprint on the surface
and turn away.

Now practiced in love,
you may advance to a lily, even
a small and simple fish.
To be sure, though, you may wish to try
another stone.

Celibate

I must have wires
instead of bones;
instead of flesh,
congealed shadow
like clay pressed
on a sculptor's study
or the pressed resin
of action figures.

A cage of angles,
I turn with a jerk,
and part crowds.
A point extending
from a finger-tip
might draw blood;
another, from a shoulder,
could summon lightning.

The Suitor Reviews His Talking Points

Because diamonds are transported
in brown paper bags.

Because a durian that goes unsold in Chicago
would be a staple in Singapore.

Because penicillin arose
from aging bread.

Because a twisted bone, too, yields marrow.

Because, knowing this,
you are worthy.

Reply

Your letter was thin,
almost transparent,
yet folded precisely
as the inner wrapper
of a Japanese rice candy

that you can peel off and let melt,
warm snowflake in the mouth,
or leave on to dissolve
with its contents
in one sweet piece.

Once, not knowing
where to begin, I tried this
with the outer wrapper.
The thick paper was unchanged,
without flavor, or sustenance—
the opposite of your few words.

Coitus

It is only flesh,
More or less the same compendium

Of water, laced
With carbon and trace minerals,

That makes up a bison's leg,
The pork on a plate.

It is only flesh
Meeting more of the same,

The means for a double helix
To spiral through time.

It is simply flesh
In an aroused state,

Soon satisfied,
Made a vessel

Of attachment, of regret, infused—
Afflicted—by what some call a spirit,

Whose noted powers
Do not include taking back

The entanglement of flesh with other flesh,
Now complex as a molecule.

Vintage

Held up to the light
like a diamond
in a jeweler's loupe,
or a candled egg,
a grape assumes the aspect
of a breast veined
by living to a certain age,
distended with a wealth
that strains the skin
as if to break out
into the wide air's caress.

Yet, as gravity
pulls that roundness
away from itself,
toward the round earth,
the stretching flesh
may still offer itself
for pleasures taken,
as reverence demands,
by pressing slowly
and with thoroughness,
and by sipping, for hours on end,
the wine of its long sacrifice.

Talking in Sleep

Songs and detective novels turn
on secrets emerging
like an answer from the Eight Ball's liquid
between snores and smoother breaths
that mean nothing but themselves,
though the premise dissolves in bedchambers
where hired subjects slumber
among electrodes and fresh linens,
saying a word or two that could be
drawn from a tourist's phrasebook.

So, asleep, we're not
the oracles that we're not, awake.
Immune to science, one keeps vigil
over a lover whose sleeping thoughts
are disclosed, at intervals,
as *car, hamburger, armchair*,
dots unconnected
and remote as the other
who dreams on, unknown.

Synopsis

Love and other fictions
would sustain him for the winter.
While, objectively, his hemisphere
was tilting from the sun,
he inhabited a greenhouse walled
and warmed by virtue of another's touch,
fruit swelling and in reach until
it seemed that tasting was his only task.
Yet branches went unpruned,
rappelling vines usurped the strongest limbs,
and weevils multiplied.
Cracks webbed the glass,
a test of every passing vandal's aim, and then
a target for a brick thrown from inside,
admitting weather and defeat
as spring's days lengthened into fact.

Epilogue

Embracing, we didn't
form an arch
and admit countless joys,

nor did we convene
like scallop's valves
around a shared, pink life.

A gentle beast simply
approached us and rolled over
to lay bare its belly and throat.

This trust called for walks in wide parks
and hand-feeding in restaurants
before we shared our bed;

this creature, needing two for warmth,
stayed with us
and never growled or snapped.

At a season's end
it left on quiet pads,
for its own animal reasons,

and we stood by ourselves,
sharing an absence
and no more.

Tableau

In a Renaissance painting
whose title I've forgotten
completely as a stronger man
would forget you,
Lucifer holds a seat
in the heavenly councils' back benches,
the way you might think of me
when I call,
untangling the telephone cord
from my horns.

Divorce

An arch over two names and bodies
snaps like a wishbone.
The one who pulled harder
gets the larger half
of the assets and the children's days
and is called fortunate.

Snowballs in August

Two seasons have intervened
since we packed the powder
tight as our eight limbs.

In the freezer, two snowballs
are joined improbably
as a trapeze artist's catch
or my parents' marriage, any marriage.
Their rightful heir, I once yawned, after love,
Credo quia absurdum est.

What I've since known of union
is that my bones knit together
without my willing them,
that the far oceans mingle.
My credo is halved: *absurdum est.*

I break off a sphere,
frangible as trust,
and enough survives my hand
to try out on a fence.

Thwack.

That one was yours.

The other will keep indefinitely,
lone and whole as a heart
in its natural state.

Handful

In my father's wisdom
you were lucky to have
a handful of friends
to confide in.

I had that handful, and overflowing
they have spilled across the map,
sifting into jobs and marriages,
the upkeep of homes,
their addictions and religions.

What's left is the hand
that hasn't grasped those things,
open to wave or beckon,
or make shadows on a wall.
Open for self-love,
the kind close by.

After Heartbreak

Daylight lengthens of its own
inaminate accord. This much is well.
There is also a greater abundance—
of hours, of the telephone's still.
For almost everyone, there is
the good fortune of a world that proceeds
as if nothing has happened.
Its surfaces, imbued with a brightness,
are neutral as a curb.
Something in them holds fast,
shows no deference to events.
One joins that something eventually,
perhaps after work, on the way to the bus stop.
Footstep after footstep
is not swallowed by the ground.
There is air enough to draw breath
and hum, then sing, "Simple Gifts"
without waiting for an audience.

2.

Reasons for Moving

A general in China wrote,
twenty-six centuries ago,
do not move without a reason for moving.

Words that last this long compel attention.
I heed them, and compile a list:

Because somewhere else, at this hour,
the sun rises or sets.
Because migrating birds can be followed.
Because the lease is up,
and another will begin.

The passport hasn't been stamped enough.
There is a woman to forget,
or thinking to be done
at a different elevation.
Because a body in motion
tends to remain in motion,
at times, in an orbit around no star.

Ozona

Land enough is sea
if it's flat enough, and wide,
not vegetated in untoward colors,
not buoying up abundant towers
and capacious stadia.

But this sea does not admit
one who would be submerged
in only minutes.
There's no sudden enfolding,
no quick escape.

Not sinking, though,
does not mean to swim.
Here there is no smooth sailing.
To arrive in good port
takes a long passage overland.
To remain, a long, committed drowning.

American Solitudes

DuSable, black and alone,
surveys a plain of bison
majestic and immune to speech.

*

A seed rattles in a crate
without touching soil or a crevice
in which to rest and unfold.

*

A man's calendar is spread across the map.
He caroms among cities and sounds.
Familiar are the jet's drone,
the murmur of the cabin's strangers.

*

A chapter begins *Think of*
two stars and the space between them
as one baseball in New York,
another in Los Angeles.

*

Some dream of owning
no more than a carload
and leaving at the thought of leaving.
They will choose destinations
less than routes—traced, retraced—
and from those tracings read
their desires' signatures.

Mortality Among Blues Men

Poisoned whiskey was the exception,
or an icepick through the eye.
The rule was the same slow killing
that closes any career—or none.
Good liquor, if it was enough
to forget a woman who was gone,
still made a liver big enough
to fill a crossroad.
Cheap meats silted arteries like backwaters,
and cigarettes, that steadied hands
to play another set or drive one more hour
to where a colored man could stay,
kept burning when the butt was snuffed,
turned thoats and lungs to damp ash
that would yield to no mojo hand.
In this way day's delta was erased,
its bayous exiled in long night,
West and South Sides leveled
by a train that came slow
and didn't look like glory.
These men saw it coming
but in spite of that, *because* of that—
Goddamn, they could play.
And they knew how to sing.

FM Badlands

Memphis has left the rearview mirror
but goes on in the DJ's voice.
He introduces a ten-year-old song as "classic"
because it is ten years old.
Its plaints and power chords address
a timeless couple,
attraction and despair.
The sponsors are wagering
this choice will wring nostalgia
from a chosen demographic,
but their broad embrace misses
those who recall from that time
no love, no adventure,
only the song itself, now setting
in a static horizon.
That absence could be filled
with prayer or wonder
that there's anything—
even this suddenly tuneless car,
in the seeming middle of nowhere—
instead of nothing,
but if there's an inner life to be had
it is set aside for the noise
that spars with the senses
and means staying awake
at seventy miles an hour.

The next station twangs loss.
Loss itself twangs, vibrating
long after the note is still,
like the rope on which a quiet farmer
hanged himself years ago.
The sound does not cease,
but is abandoned for futures.
At noon August soybeans and cotton are trading,
as is their wont, before giving way

to silence, then instrumental waves:

tunes strained through a dozen string sections
and a single tempo, followed by
the "Heroic Polonnaise"—
a college, and its station,
can appear anywhere,
like an overlapping signal's voice
that echoes in a near-empty studio
and makes every day the Sabbath,
every radio a church
proclaiming Resurrection
without Crucifixion, the Word
as preached in Guatemala
by spring-break missionaries,
all smiles and Bibles,
who haven't lost an adult tooth
or a village.
Text and sermon conclude at the dial's end
with a choir made up of whale-song,
theramin, the music of the spheres.

Another lap of the dial starts,
and the drive's first song fades in,
desire, power chords, an endless hook,
nostalgia for when the day's sounds
were still unknown, and a foretaste
of what lies ahead: minutes later,
with its own DJs, Jackson comes into sight.

Post-Prairie

The tall grasses have receded to points,
those points receding,
taking with them the bison—
a defeat offset
by no reaction dreamed in physics,
the tall grasses' absence
measured in relief, their yielding
only to discs and blades
like hooves of a dire beast
from the Prophets,
replaced by neither low lawns
nor glades of corn in shallow-rooted rows—
stalks broken, like weak wills, in one season.

Humid Continental

I could take a handful of this air
and squeeze out
a train of raindrops.

But that would take effort.

It is better to let moisture
work its way into things,
sheets of paper that curl
at the corners and revert
to ancestral scrolls,

a wooden door swelling
in its swollen doorjamb.

To open that door and walk out
would take a hard pull,
an act of will.

But it is better
to let unfurl from the wood

small, then greater fungi
shaped like trumpets and like drums.

Someone should attend their still recital.

Work Site

A hill is laid open
at the property line—
the grass shorn sideways,
and the broad-leaf weeds,
tap and matted roots
edged at the humus.
Lower horizons are laid bare
at a sudden canyon's wall:
loam shading into sand and clay,
and below, condensed from forests and reefs
the greater densities of stone.

Until a retaining wall
is made to stand in
for the missing buttress of earth,
the layered epochs can be read
as lines of a text.

If its sense does not emerge at once,
the soil is not at fault.

Lawn Pastoral

We might say that squirrels,
gathering acorns, flourish tails
that conduct a score taken up
by cardinals as they chirp and lay in
grams of fat against the winter;
and we might observe, from the porch,
how life persists even
as October lowers on the year.
Surplus flesh and foliage, shed
like hairs in a comb,
don't diminish life in general—
with a capital L—
ground of proverbs
and vehicle of genes.

Outside, particular lives prolong
their interval above the dust.
The longer life of their species
provides no forage, no cover
unless a code is found
that, crossing species,
will explain it to the sparrows
scattered by a landing crow.
Explain it to the rabbits mown in two.

Briefing

The day issues its imperatives,
but not to you,
who have nothing to bring
to this table in time.
Perhaps you did yesterday, or last week.
In theory you might someday have,
again, some bearing on events,
like the heavyweight
who comes out of retirement
in spite of popular demand,
or the Anglo-Saxon badass
who is summoned once more,
on the strength of his resume,
to fight a monster in a swamp.
This could happen,
as a satellite fragment
expected to fall north of Tuvalu
might land on your recently purchased used car.

Your role today, though, is to stand and wait,
or better, sit in a corner booth.
Yours is the work of the homely friend,
who, when the others get asked to dance
and have a chance of getting laid,
watches the coats and purses,
makes sure nothing's slipped in the drinks.
The coats, the purses, the drinks
would probably be just fine,
but this fictitious sense of mission
is conferred by the well-favored
in a preemptive strike against their guilt.
Theirs is the same impulse that takes from your pocket
the quarter you won't really miss
and sets it in the cracked palm
of the panhandler it won't really help.

Thus now you are kept in the notional loop.
It's too much trouble
to have a temp delete your name
from the databases, the mailing lists.
You have no stake in leaks or trial balloons.
Your Rolodex holds the cards of those retired or deceased.
You know that you don't know
the secret handshake—or if there is one.
As some confess murder to the comatose patient,
the golden elect see no harm
in sloughing off their burden of consciousness
onto you, a terminal twig on a phone tree,
or dropping off a sheaf of print-outs,
topped with a yellow adhesive note
that reads, in a neat but relaxed hand, *FYI*.

The memos state insider trading
will begin at one p.m.
The board of directors has refuted Marx:
to oppress the proletariat would entail
having contact with them.
An Indian casino on the other side of the country
will next week make its slots the loosest in the world,
and thousands more will come to imagine,
as you once did,
that when they pull a lever, it will count.

Aurora's Lockers

Aurora's lockers wait for me.
At universities where I studied,
staying out of town, at hotel pools,
the numbered plates are stamped with one place
in Denver, Washington, New Orleans.
Underlined with ventilation shark-slits,
they read "homeboy" in sheet metal.
Sheet metal. In shop class
we learned to bend that oxymoron:
my boxes crumpled.
I had to make a living
with no skill in my hands,
and I followed the lockers, as far as they went.

East High and West High pour together
new ex-rivals every June
to spot-weld prisms around space
that will outlast layoffs and the Lyon Metal plant.
The doors shut tight as marriage in the Church.
Hooks and latches bolt down
with imagined suits, plane tickets, passports,
ghosts of calling cards in law and floristry.
The seams are pressed, the rivets driven fast
by retold stories of bats, cleats, helmets
from lockers left in town.
Homeboy. The door slams, the slotted dark swallows
my layers of notebooks, neckties, and tweed.

My laps run around Aurora.
Back or forth is the farthest I swim away.
Showered, I stand and work a combination,
down to my name and wet footprints,
facing an enclosure I've always known.

3.

Concordance to Thought

The slender word *I* leads all entries.
God appears all too rarely,
sex, with undue frequency;
both, seldom on one page.
Bread abounds,
and *bead*'s almost beyond counting,
though a *newel*, too,
crops up now and then, or a *zygote*
such as I used to be.
Armadillo's occur for no practical purpose,
like the *pomegranate*'s that,
most autumns, I forget to buy,
and the *artichoke*
one can, but shouldn't, live without.
Death falls between enemy and friend.
Resignation mounts,
luck comes in streaks,
and *joy* arises for no particular reason
while throughout, reflecting on the rest,
is *wonder*.

An Afternoon

A man of clay I
walked my dogs of dust
past trees leaved
with future humus
crossing clay
such as steadies oaks' roots
and dirt that breaks out
into dogs or a man
who would browse
on the dark earth's mushrooms,
having worked up an appetite
with walking and cliches

There was also a sun
and winds
of disparate agendas
bearing their respective
presentiments without stopping
here to offer
a traveler's tale

every speck and motion
a parenthesis to the rest
all unenclosed
as far as the eye can see

Hands

With only slight arms
to restrain them,
my hands might lift up
with a will of their own
like twin dirigibles,
paired swallows,
buoys recovering from a wake,
or as if resting
on a lectern of dough,
thick with yeast,
rising to take strength,
perhaps another hand,
the rung of a ladder
hidden in the air.

street preacher

takes up his corner
as the hookers
go to breakfast
lifts a black block of scripture
and exhales at the top
of god-given lungs
the verses he knows
from all sixty-six books
as essential for saving
dog walkers and bike couriers
newsstand clerks and florists
who find his voice and volume
his outstretched arms
unblinking eyes incidental
as shrink-wrap
while he overflows
all day with mission and converts
not a soul

To a Martyr for His People

You wanted something besides
day labor and the prospect of arrest.
You wanted to be part of something
larger than yourself, enduring.
At seventeen, you have succeeded.
The earth is great.
It will hold you for all time.

Chest X-Ray

The dark spot is likened to a cloud.
The surrounding lightness—a diminished sky.
Below are a figure, and adjacent figures,
objects of the coming rain.

Sweater

This wool is the closest I can come
to the distant fold's
fellow-feeling, winter warmth.

But I may yet know
a claw's election,
the raw entry of teeth.

Everywhere, wolves must be fed.

Bequest

Give my name, little used,
to fellowships at a college
I did not attend,
to a pellucid one-celled form
that, with particular grace, navigates
a drop of pond water.

Dysthymia

Bounding squirrels that won't
stop and find themselves
beneath the weight of thought.
The warm rising that, today,
won't be satisfied within the law.
Taste, any taste—
the brown flavor of bran or coffee,
the same as peaches, milk and gin.
Trains and passengers
at appointed hours,
on predestined rails.
For these the heart keeps beating.

After Housework

The laundry is folded,
the porcelain purified.
Not even a tumbler
rests in the sink.

Dust is banished.

Every surface gleams completely
as a fresh headstone.

An End

Suicide comes of a morning
that is otherwise nondescript.
There's still coffee in the can,
some money in the bank.
There is only, relentlessly, the day,
and the prospect of more just like it.
Their mocking light could go on
indefinitely, illuminating
exclusions from countless guest lists,
the space outside of velvet ropes
and thick windows, closed to no one else,
unless measures of the strongest kind are taken.
The opponent days must be struck down for all time,
before they conquer by sheer force of numbers.

Toward a Eulogy

How do we say that someone
no longer serves our purposes,
failing to pick up the telephone,
no longer meeting for drinks?

The soul, if there was one,
has lifted away.

The cells have lapsed
from holding back
the world at large.
They are being taken into other cells.

How can we punish
the flesh that ignores us,
except to banish it from our presence

with shoveled earth, or flames,
a choked railing
at one who won't rise to reply?

Prescription

A small clatter—
the floor swarms with scarabs
weighing the same as paperclips
or a body on hands and knees
scouring over tiles, in corners,
around stool and cantilevered cabinet
to retrieve one capsule,
then the next:
a day, and another day.

For Bad Wine

Once in a field, in a wide rising stretch of paintbrush
& purple vetch, we stuck down

a tent, like punctuation, and drank through the evening
our bottle of bad wine.

—Kate Northrop

Because the stores where finer wines are sold
are closed, or too far away to drive
on a rainy night, and because,
truth be told, we're already a bit tipsy,
we'll settle for what we can find in town.

Because the bottles of dusty neck and shoulders
that suggest long aging, and a high price,
lie on their sides on a rack
too low to reach without stooping,
we'll take one of the bright bottles
that stand close by.

Since so many of the labels are written
in strange languages that bring no comfort,
we narrow down to the plain-spoken domestics.

As, even in mid-life, we're intimidated
by the corkscrew, the very cork,
the intricate and solemn techniques
and auguries of its removal,
we look among the simple screw tops,
such as we turned to open soda and juice
before our first high school drink.

Because we may as well toast our younger selves
who didn't know Boone's Farm from Bordeaux,
who knew we would get rich while doing good,
but in the meantime had to scrimp,

we will take the cheapest brand.

Because we now know better,
but have to save for retirement,
we will take the large and cost-effective jug.

Because we have our reasons
and don't want to tell them again,
we'll refill our glasses
and drain every drop.

4.

As Art Springs from a Wound

There's no need to stay up, planning death,
or push away full plates.
No need for the other symptoms,
the familiar list,
because a pill dissolves them.
Then nothing's good or bad
but thinking makes it so,
and nothing's that bad when there's the will
to write a letter, even post it,
and begin another, asking a friend
what if salesmen—of anything—are right,
and, with them, cheerleaders,
the evangelists of tall hair,
the televised prophets of real estate?
What if all is bounty,
for the taking with a smile?
Then all art and craft
is happenstance and shining scar,
canopy over a ground of grief
that gives way, toppling statues,
symphonies, and poems.

All these years we could have been taking sun.
We should have been making money.
But we didn't, and must count it loss.
Pale and broke, we settle for beauty.

After Psalm 22:14

I am poured out like water
cooling cats' paws
rinsing off the curb's urine
before meeting a ditch
then a river
to buoy grain barges
shape myself to their hulls
before evaporating into
the clouds' zoo of shapes
raining on crops and weeds
I roll off furrows
supporting waves of skaters
insulating beneath them
the somnolent fish

Full Stop

The full stop will inherit the earth.
The sentence its tolerated prelude,
the abbreviation foreshadows its ambition.

Though small, like
the far end of a mineshaft
or a funnel cloud's distant tip,

this dry pool
will cover epochs.

Collapsing Barn

The boards bow, the roof saddles
as if the air's weight
pressed them into ruins,
or an architecture of compassion
where cross-eyed owls
haunt the blasted rafters
above dry cows, a stuttering bachelor
who bales hay, the pitchfork's tines
splayed wildly, like hope.

The Fallen Twig

The fallen twig is not thanked
for being itself
instead of a snake
or a poison-tipped umbrella,

but cursed for being
underfoot, interrupting
a lawn's otherwise
perfect green.

This singular confluence
of xylem and phloem,
small sap, slender bark,
may be chosen
for a sparrow's essential nest,
daubed and wattled
against a cotton swab, tinsel,
dryer lint, where another twig
could serve as well.

No higher praise will be given
the fallen twig, its end
a point of departure for the distance
between what should be
and what, relentlessly, is.

Unseen

1.
Among smaller species
in a drop of water,
one paramecium rotates,
absorbing its path.

2.
A tree falls in Amazonia
without an echo.

3.
Where Earth's dust settles
a mountain grows
higher than air.

4.
A fourth thing.

Water Wants

What we want water to do is stay
right where we want it to, then
come on sharp command
like an overtrained dog
at our lips' beck, our plumbing's call.
Hence Hoover Dam.
Even if we want wisely,
water has other things to do,
water things, like keeping salt dissolved
and Atlantis lost, water things
like steaming uselessly off Sonoran rocks,
cutting canyons through the eons' earth,
washing away the unjust with the just.
If water didn't do them, they wouldn't get done.

Pistachios

Clams of dry land,
suspended mid-gape,
they are, as well, truncated
busts of hatchlings that peep
for an imminent feeding,
and parentheses, poised
to shelter a digression,
which ends

in the closure of hands
that extract the meat,
casting the shells,
light as images,
onto a midden,
into the wind.

The Drowned Fish

for Vladimir Trendafilov

One surfaces from time to time,
intact, with no tumor
of industry or age—
a moist tablet on which
is written the diagnosis
that the specimen could not withstand
its native element.

How this happens is still unknown.
A possibility that bears considering,
in *Nature* or *Science,*
is how a being might evolve
slightly away from its habitat,
with a fin uselessly lengthened for traction,
a misplaced drive to gasp for air.

This process might explain
the eyes dimming behind windshields
and before bright screens,
or a pedestrian's sudden reach
inside his coat, though he doesn't
withdraw a wallet
or step into a store.
He could be searching, then, for a nascent flap of gill
or feel, chafing in his sleeve, a new feather.

Arboreal

Blue Hawaiis have nothing to do with this tree.
And whiskey sours have nothing to do with tree.
Nor shrimp cocktails, nor cocktail franks,
or the entree to follow.
They leave this tree unaffected.
The price of salt approaches
neither bark nor root.
Likewise, futures in copper or corn,
and the corn itself, and cornrows
across Iowa or a scalp.
Breezes have more bearing on these leaves.

No less remote
from this forest of parsimony
is whether a given man and woman's
want coincide in each other.

Whole disciplines of the academy
bend no branch or twig.
Ages' and conquerors' stilled axes
never touched this trunk,
and Lee Harvey Oswald, alone
or with others,
never enjoyed this shade.
The rest of matter was committed
to other niches, other names.
The remaining space
could only be filled by this tree,
this inevitable tree.

The Jazz Clock

The jazz clock ticks
sometimes, when it wants to,
and sometimes it tocks.
Now and then,
for the sheer sake of variety,
it both ticks and tocks
like its wall and mantle brethren
in the customary alliteration.
Just not for long.

Instead, the jazz clock measures one moment,
then the next, like
the long tidal pull of a sleeper's breath,
the lightning in a sneeze,
the last eternal seconds before a night of love begins
and the instant that it lasts.

This timepiece, too, starts and stops
with morning traffic
that snakes from block to block,
gridlocks, then syncopates and pulls over
for several measures' rest, making way
for the siren solo of an ambulance
whose passenger's heart has dropped
its immaterial drumsticks;

but just as fast as that traffic jammed
the jam dissolves—
first with a spurt of pent-up momentum,
then with an artery's steady flow.
The jazz clock slows with the thought
of an expanding universe,
the earth's lengthening lap around the sun
and its gears slip, like a deep-space probe,
toward meeting with an infinite still
until, on an African savannah,

a most immediate
cheetah accelerates
from zero to sixty
in pursuit of an appetizing gazelle
and closes the distance,
pouncing
as a prophet in another hemisphere
is suddenly encompassed
by a light he knows,
this time, is not a seizure.

The hour hand leaps ahead,
the minute hand pulls back as if to clap,
and the stunned second hand oscillates
while existence tucks in its shirt, then moves on
to the crowing of a rooster,
the trilling of a robin or
some other kind of pizzicato bird.

The jazz clock, consequently, has no alarm.
It is always time to wake up.
It is always time to dream.

Biography

J.D. Smith has published one previous collection of poems, *The Hypothetical Landscape*, and the edited anthology *Northern Music: Poems About and Inspired by Glenn Gould*. His poetry, fiction, essays and reviews appear in journals in the United States, Canada and Great Britain. Born in Aurora, Illinois, he currently lives and works as an editor and writer in Washington, DC.

Printed in the United States
34311LVS00007B/310-432

9 781933 456058